LOVE'S VENOM

A COLLECTION OF POEMS

L. Virgilio

BookLeaf
Publishing

India | USA | UK

Presentation by *BookLeaf Publishing*

Web: www.bookleafpub.com

E-mail: info@bookleafpub.com

ISBN: 9789358360318

First edition 2021

To the Bitches who betrayed me
and the cunts who tried to play me;
Thank you for inspiring my
muse

PREFACE

A powerful dedication for a book filled with hard emotions. Each of these poems were written about various situations in my life, but they come together to tell of one specific moment .

In the winter of 2018, my favorite person in the whole world got cancer. And instead of staying at my side, the Keeper of My Heart turned into a Ghost. While I remained steady and true to my Favored throughout their disease, I realized just how much I *hated* my Ex. How Love had turned into this toxic, poisonous thing.

This is that narrative, in poem form. And the story ends the same way that relationship eventually did; with one final set of words.

Each smile you
Give me melts a
Little bit more
Of my frozen
Heart.

I want you
But I hesitate
Because
I know pain
More than
I know love
And I fear
The Unknown

My Hips
Your Hands
A beat between us

My neck
Your Teeth
A mark for Later

My kiss
Your Taste
a Pyre of heat

My hair
Your pull
An accelerant

My need
Your want
And even exchange.

I could write in
Every language,
use every word,
yet still never
describe
you
or
my feelings for
you

The softest parts
of Me
Can only be seen
In your arms

I wanted to punch
A hole through your chest
To grab your heart.
But when I did
I found nothing but sand
That slipped through my fingers.
I hide my tears of
disappointment
At finding you a sack
of pulverized stone.
That, once opened,
became nothing
But a hollowed out burlap bag.
Because Life beat you down
before I could get to you.
So when I asked for your heart,
You didn't know that you were
Already too broken to save.

Foolish.
You were Wrong in all
The Right ways.
Corruption
Laid out for me in a Maze.
A Puzzle for me to try out.
To uncover what you're about.
Found you to be
Malicious instead
Of soulfully nutritious
Learned you were poison:
Bitter anguish the reason
I became toxic with just one hit.
Corrupted myself just to get lit.
Burnt myself out just to please
you
Tempered myself and became
Subdue.

Be careful
Who you take as your King
For
Spineless men
Crumble under the
weight of a
Crown

New Years, I asked
'Please Stay' – And you did;
While it was soft,
While it was *easy*
Then she got cancer
I unraveled, drowning;
Reaching out for you
And your hand
You reached back
Fingers brushed
So close
Only to Vanish
You withdrew
Let me succumb
Alone
Under the wave of grief

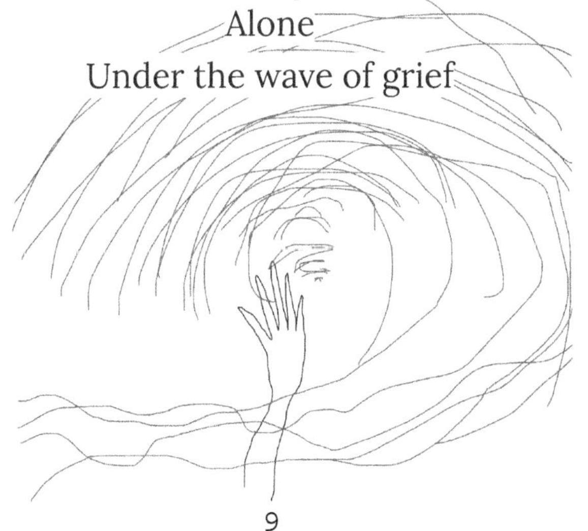

Contorted Pain

Teeth Crack
Breathing Stops
Eyes Wide
Skin Waxy
and yet still outsiders whisper
"It's a Sin"
They look at the manifestation of
agony
in my loved one
Only to spill acid upon them,
Demanding they commune with
torture.
What kind of faith demands that?
I want no part.
Take your faith and words
out of my life.
Your false empathy is unwelcomed
here.
-*Justified Suicide*

One day
My love won't be enough.
The pain will be stronger,
Harder to ignore.
And me being there
won't register
as *enough.*
On that Day
I'll lose you

Forever

Car Rides filled with silence
Answers we never wanted to get
next steps feel forever off
Cries I'll have to hide
Echos of a time we've done this
before
Really didn't need to take after your
mother
Stages make no sense
talks I'm too young to have
All of a sudden the world looks
different
gorgeous days counted
One day, this too shall pass
but I'm not ready for how it'll end

Some People
Can't bare to say the words
Can't even hear them.
They resonate too loudly in their
souls
So I take them all
I take:
Cancer
Prognosis
Chemo
Radiation
Life Expectancy
Stages.
And I let them tear through my
emotions
Ruin everything in me
Then I pack them up
I sow them into these words
Embedded them into my stories
Force those words to echo through
pages
Cause if they exist there

Then maybe
just *maybe*,
they won't exist in my life anymore.

Familiar scents
Of
Fresh Antiseptic and Stale
Death.
Hardness of Plastic chairs and
Bottled Emotions
All Familiar
All Numbing
People crying
Agonizing moans
I sit,
wait,
suffer
Waiting for answers
Waiting for solutions
Powerless
Knowing it's a countdown
Time Ticks on
I wait
For The End.

Grief isn't a monster
Rather it makes
Humans into Monsters
By
Destroying the
Shackles of humanity
Which binds the beast
That lives in the
Heart of man.

She is the First rain after a drought
You are poison on prize-winning
Roses
Her death would leave me
inconsolable
Yours would barely register
She is my Favorite
I get to see her in Technicolor
While she only showed you shades
of Rose
To me, I've seen her in grief and in
fear of death
You only see her when things are
good
You run away, while I remain
She is to me a mother
To you a woman you barely want to
acknowledge as *Ma'*
You skated off to parts unknown
Until I stepped back
And now you're bitter.
Hateful

Angry at me.
Yet, she lives because I remained
You had freedom
while I cared for her in all her
moods
I may be the villain in your story
But she remained in that story
cause of me.
And it wasn't for you
but for *me*.

Grief is that one guest, the one that
lingers well passed polite.
So you have to grin and find the
energy to continue
To entertain them
When you want to clean up after
the party, take off your lovely outfit
and make up.
Yet, Grief doesn't take the hint.
Doesn't know when to leave.
So you remain in that state –
In your beautiful outfit, in your
painted face, grinning and bearing
the Guest that won't leave.
Cause Grief has its own time table
And you have no say in it.
And even when Grief leaves, it just
becomes a ghost.
One that haunts us forever.
But it's never the person that died
that haunts us
Rather

It's the *What If's*
The *What could have been's*
The sudden longing for moments
we can't have
For the memories we face with
bluer emotions
It's the lingering scar on our hearts
From where they were cut from us
Grief is a Ghost that haunts us
But at least we know we loved
enough to have those ghosts.
Grief is an emotion that lingers
well passed polite.

Through hard times
True colors shine out:
The Strong hold fast
And
The Weak Bow out.
The weak are for the
Good Times
When things are
Rose and Golden Light
The strong are for the
Dark Times
When the ground's barren
And
You're looking for a fight.
There's nothing wrong
With weak friends
You just don't
show struggle to them;
They'd never understand.

They demand to know your
secrets;
To know your pains.
They get off on knowing you've
been hurt.
That your skin and heart are
scarred.
They reach out like greedy, spoiled
children,
fingers ruddy from their own
slights.
Ready to mix their own pain in with
yours.
So they can claim you.
Dip their pain into the fresh blood
of your reopened wounds;
So they can hold it over you,
Whisper about it with others,
so they can claim
to know your pain.
That you were less damaged than
them

That you were less broken than
them
They want to revel in your pain yet
undermine it.
Huffy and disgusted is how they act
when they don't get it.
Like candy denied to them, how
dare you keep your scars hidden.
How dare you deny them their
show,
Their entertainment,
Their sick pleasure.
-A *Victim Voyeur*

"Be Happy"
They Whisper
As if Positivity
Will Make it all Better
But it's a Bandaid
Underneath, The wound
Still exists
Just Covered
So you don't have
To see it.

They are just for me;
My feelings
I can get caught up in them
Tangled in them
Hung up in them.
Hidden from Prying Eyes
I feel Love,
Compassion,
Empathy,
Anguish,
and Pain.
Yet all you'll ever see is
Amusement,
Disinterest,
Detachment.
Because
They are not for you
They are just for me.
I'm not unfeeling,
I'm just not on
Display

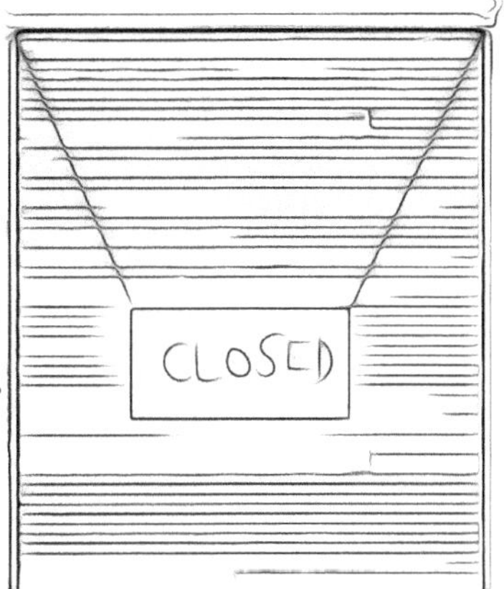

My mom says:
"Be Understanding"
"Be Kind"
"Be Forgiving"
I respond:
"I wish I were a better person."
But I'm not.
I'm not built that way.
I got fangs and venom,
Claws and Jowls
I try to be like them–
Sweet,
Compassionate,
Kind.
But I've got a darkness in me
Predatory instincts
That are hard to temper.
I wish I were a better person.
But I'm *not*.

"Good-Bye"
Short and Sweet.
Is that a promise?
Make sure it is.
Make sure your face is never
seen again.
Make sure you keep gone.
There is no:
"Welcome Back"
There is no
Repairing this
That was a
Molotov Cocktail
To all your bridges
Make sure
You make peace with your choice.
And
Don't look back.
Because I won't.

It's swirls in my gut:
A black storm of rage and disgust
Hatred thunders across my mind,
As lightning crackles along my
tongue.
While I hold the hurricane at bay,
It beats and screams in my chest
Demanding to be able
to lay waste to that
which created it.

Say My Name
Say it in a whisper
Say it in a scream
Say it with Love
Say it with Hate
Say it to my *face*
Say it behind my *back*
But know
It'll always get back to me
So if you wanna talk shit
It's best to keep my name
out of your mouth
Call me
She-Who-Must-Not-Be-Named
That way you won't have to
explain
Why my name escaped your lips
Because my hands don't have
ears
When it comes to correcting
your lies.

Keep my Name out of Your Mouth
I heard my name's been going
South
Heard it exiting from your mouth
A detour on it's way to Glory
Pulled out for your bullshit story
It's gotta be that time of year
When you start hating out of fear
Coming for people out of your
league
Trying to spill some tea
But I'd hate to remind you of your
place
But now it's time to place my Ace:
You're but a footnote in my story,
Barely enough to take inventory
You couldn't just let me go
Now trying to tarnish my glow
Couldn't just let me be
Gotta flex all your immaturity
Complaining now that it hurt
That I peaced out and kicked up
dirt
Left you in the dust

Not wanting to deal with your
distrust
Boo who, like it wasn't your fault
Like you didn't come at me full
assault
Well go spread those lies
And send your spies
Because I'll be working
While you'll be hurting
For they say it takes two to tango
But nine times out of ten, it's one
just trying to tangle
Maybe next time
In you pastime
You'll think before you speak
Least I have to prove you meek

Some of you were told
You are Queens
But weren't taught how
To act like One:
And it Shows.

Hands grab ankles
"Repent"
They decry, yanking down
"Regret"
They Sneer, jerking to the
ground
"Remorse"
They mock.
But
Kick Free!
Watch them fall.
Returning to their level
Returning to the middle.
Sit at the Top,
Breath.
Then Climb on.

You tried to be a flower
Petals hiding thorns
Then you saw pressed flowers
in the pages of my favorite books

You tried to be a viper
coiled to strike
Yet your fangs hit my boots
Handmade and Snake Skin.

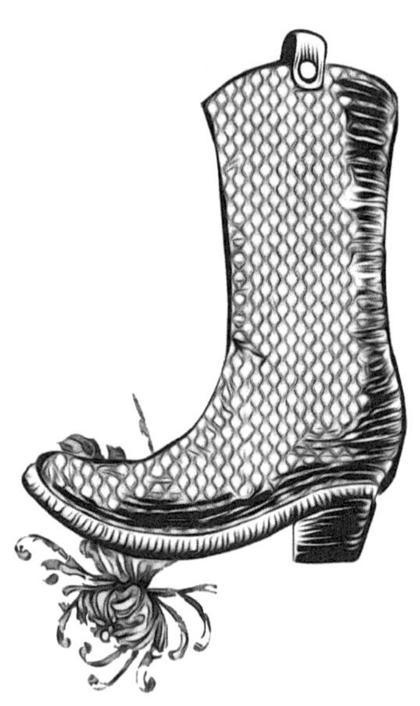

Your knife's at my back
Your smile's at my front
Damocles' Sword above my head
Do I step towards
Your deceptive smile?
Or back into your treacherous
blade?
The Choice leaves me Divided.
The Sword Falls.

My needle had purple thread this time
My frayed seams expose stuffing,
another round as a chew toy
My Ragdoll body a borage of colorful
threads
Some years old, Some months old
All colorful, All *distracting*
So no one can see how often I'm
wounded;
Beaten Down
So I don't have to answer
"Are you okay?"
Because if I show
Strength, Resilience, and Fortitude
Then maybe others can draw on them
from me.
So I stitch
Myself back together
Ready for the Next round

I don't care
Enough about the
Opinions of fools
To give wings
to words that
They'll never
Deserve.
*-To those who say my poems are
about them*

To the Selfish
WE is just a twisted
And flipped version of
ME.

"We're Still here"
They whisper, reaching out to
the broken
Without Fear
"We're still beside you"
They know nothing
Yet still, they care
Still look beyond to see
Not a monster
Not a victim
No a side
But a person
Who they call Friend.
Cherish those-
For they are Rare.
-True Friends

It wasn't the distance
Between us that
Killed me.
It was the
Silence
that filled it

Normally I have so many words.
Normally I have a grip of how to
Put words to Situations
Words to Feelings
Words to events
Yet
Now I am without them
Now all I can do
Is figure out
How to continue
With a vast silence
That has created such
A yawning chasm in my life
I think
For one
I just need to turn and
Walk away
Back to my dwelling
To learn to appreciate
The Silence once more
For life is always
Full of the hardest lessons

Cause I thought I knew
What betrayal was.
Thought I knew
The depth some
Will go to hurt others.
Thought I knew
The darkest parts of humanity.
I was wrong
I wish I hadn't been.
I guess that's what hurts the
most:
It isn't the *wound*
It's *who* inflicted it
But the trick is
To never left them
have the chance
to do it *again*.
-*Disloyalty*

I chase
After the Future
To Leave
You in the Past

As I lie here
I think of you.
Of the moments between us
Of how we embraced
Of how we had it all.
The potential for greatest.
The first blush.
Of becoming blinded by
Your brightness
Sun spots
Blocking out the danger,
Hiding the Adder
About your neck.
Whispering poison.
Killing what could have been.
I moved back
Cause
    Antivenom is rare,
        So is a snake that doesn't strike

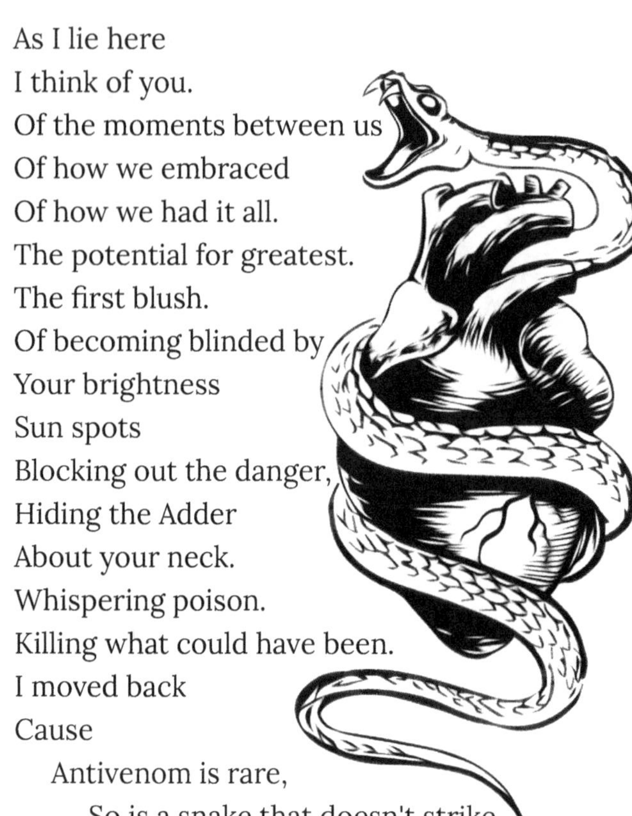

Your memory came
From nowhere
An errant thought that
Interrupted my Solace.
A reawakened yearing bloomed in
my chest,
Left me breathless under
it's weight.
I confessed out loud.
Spoke your name... to myself.
Rolled the C over my tongue
reverently,
carried the S to
prolong the taste.
I came close to
breaching the
Chasm between us.
Close
But then I remembered
It's a man made by your hand.
And yet I wrote poems
Like you'd see them
Like you'd be like me,
Scrounging for breadcrumb

pieces of my life.
Then I realized;
why would you?
I kept your name so closer to my
heart
That I made you a mystery
I made you able to hide.
No one who reads this will know You.
So I strip you of your veil -
Before You, I thought I knew love
Before You, I never questioned
myself
Before You, my path was clear
Before You, everything made sense
That was before You, Chris.
B.C
Now everything is, After You
A.C
After You, I learned what love felt like
After You, I learned what
heartbreak was
After You,
The World was a little grayer

I still have
The Ring
It's alongside:
The Sleepless Nights
The Longing
The Love.
The Insanity
The cheating
The Lies
The Threats of Suicide
The Lost time
The Falling back together
The Heartbreak
The Loss of Self.
Our End.
Most of all
It's alongside
The Romantic
I used to be.

Heartless
I removed it long ago
for it didn't
know love
only pain

It used to only beat for
Those who made me an option.
For
The Emotionally Unavailable
Or
The Broken

So I put it down
In rich soil
with chrysanthemum seeds.
I'm Heartless now
While I wait for the flowers to grow

Bravery Caused me to reach out,
Olive Branch in hand.
Found my heart beat steady.
Your response
Sounded like Dove wings
Batting away the last questions.
Found poppies in gentle queries.
Found peonies in
The soft goodbyes.
But the most of all
growing in place of destructive
fiery passion are
Soft Pastel Chrysanthemums.

I've penned
Millions of words
Seeking solace
In the space between them
But found Salvation
In its stead

-*Finally Peace*